a MEMORY *Journal*

Goodbye

That Remembered Day

Hearing the news

_____

_____

_____

_____

_____

_____

_____

_____

_____

_____

_____

_____

$\mathcal{L}$AST THINGS

Words, Thoughts, Conversations, Feelings, Moments

MEMORIAL SERVICE

The day, The ceremony, People, Music, What filled my mind and heart

KINDNESSES

Cards, Gifts, Gestures

Received   Acknowledged

_____   _____

_____   _____

_____   _____

_____   _____

_____   _____

_____   _____

_____   _____

_____   _____

_____   _____

_____   _____

Received   Acknowledged

_____   _____

_____   _____

_____   _____

_____   _____

_____   _____

_____   _____

_____   _____

_____   _____

_____   _____

_____   _____

_____   _____

_____   _____

_____   _____

If You Could Hear my Heart Today...

Dear _____ , Date _____

_____

_____

_____

_____

_____

_____

_____

_____

_____

_____

_____

_____

_____

How do I Express all I am Feeling?

I am numb...

I still can't believe it...

I am so sad...

I am mad...

I have regrets...

I wish I would have told you...

I feel guilty...

I feel vulnerable...

ALTERED REALITY

The rest of the world is going about its business as usual as though no one's world has been shattered beyond recognition.

I feel like hiding...

I'm not sure people know how to relate to me right now...

I feel lonely in my strange new world of grief...

OPING

This is what I need from my friends right now...

And what I don't...

The things that bring me comfort are...

Good Days, Bad Days

Reflections on the Journey

Good days, Bad days, Changeable moods,
Unpredictable feelings, Gratitude, Disappointments

_____

_____

_____

_____

_____

_____

_____

_____

_____

_____

_____

_____

My Questions

Where are you now? Do you see me?
Are you peaceful? Do you miss me?

_____

_____

_____

_____

_____

_____

_____

_____

_____

_____

_____

_____

Reminders of my Loss

Days on the calendar, Seasons, People,
Songs, Scents, Seemingly inconsequential things

When I See you in my Dreams

What you say, Where we are, What I remember when I awake

IF YOU COULD HEAR MY HEART TODAY...

Dear _____ , Date _____

_____

_____

_____

_____

_____

_____

_____

_____

_____

_____

_____

_____

Random Musings

Favorite Memories

Remembering your Favorite Things

Places, Passions, Hobbies, Music, Clothes, Songs, Food, Jokes, TV shows

And not so favorite things...

My Favorite Photos

Why, How I feel when I look at them...

$\mathcal{T}$REASURED KEEPSAKES

"Stuff" I will never part with...

Healing

How Time is Healing my Heart

New perspectives, Feelings, How I am changing

_____

_____

_____

_____

_____

_____

_____

_____

_____

_____

_____

_____

$\mathcal{L}$AUGHTER

It has been so long, How it feels to laugh...

Remembering what made you laugh...

Honoring your Memory

Things I am doing to celebrate your life

CONVERSATION

If we could talk today, this is what I'd say...

_____

_____

_____

_____

_____

_____

_____

_____

_____

_____

_____

_____

Rediscovering Joy

My heart is finally making room for joy.
These are the good things about life right now...

I have resolved to....

But sadness still creeps in when...

If You Could Hear my Heart Today...

Dear _____ , Date _____

_____

_____

_____

_____

_____

_____

_____

_____

_____

_____

_____

_____

_____

_____

Days
to
Remember

Friday

Saturday 1

8

7

15

6

14

22

5

13

21

29

Your Birthday

Thoughts, Feelings, How old you'd be, What I did to honor you...

The Anniversary Date of your Death

Thoughts, Feelings, What I did to honor you...

Other Significant Days